Bibliographic information published by the German National Library:

The German National Library lists this publication in the National Bibliography; detailed bibliographic data are available on the Internet at http://dnb.dnb.de .

Imprint:

Copyright © 2016 GRIN Verlag
Print and binding: Books on Demand GmbH, Norderstedt Germany
ISBN: 9783668709287

This book at GRIN:

https://www.grin.com/document/426829

Rohan Ahmed

Data mining techniques in financial fraud detection

GRIN Verlag

GRIN - Your knowledge has value

Since its foundation in 1998, GRIN has specialized in publishing academic texts by students, college teachers and other academics as e-book and printed book. The website www.grin.com is an ideal platform for presenting term papers, final papers, scientific essays, dissertations and specialist books.

Visit us on the internet:

http://www.grin.com/

http://www.facebook.com/grincom

http://www.twitter.com/grin_com

HOCHSCHULE HEILBRONN / Heilbronn University

University of technology, economy and computer science

Course Business Informatics (WIN)

Seminar Thesis – IT Management and Compliance

Literature Review

on

Data mining techniques in financial fraud detection

by

Rohan Ahmed

in

SUMMER SEMESTER 2016

Contents

List of Abbreviations

ANN   Artificial Neural Networks

CART   Classification and Regression Tree

DT   Decision Tree

DM   Data Mining

DMG   Data Mining Group

GMDH   Group Method of Data Handling

LR   Logistic Regression

MLP   Multi-Layer Perceptron

MLFF   Multi-Level Feed Forward Network

PNN   Probabilistic Neural Network

SVM   Support Vector Machine

List of tables

1. Introduction

In this seminar thesis you will get a view about the Data Mining techniques in financial fraud detection. Financial Fraud is taking a big issue in economical problem, which is still growing. So there is a big interest to detect fraud, but by large amounts of data, this is difficult. Therefore, many data mining techniques are repeatedly used to detect frauds in fraudulent activities. Majority of fraud area are Insurance, Banking, Health and Financial Statement Fraud. The most widely used data mining techniques are Support Vector Machines (SVM), Decision Trees (DT), Logistic Regression (LR), Naives Bayes, Bayesian Belief Network, Classification and Regression Tree (CART) etc. These techniques existed for many years and are used repeatedly to develop a fraud detection system or for analyze frauds.

1.1. Goals

The main object of this study is to analyze the literature in reference to Data Mining techniques for financial fraud detection with the focus on Insurance, Health, Banking and Financial Statement Fraud areas.

1.2. Structure of seminar thesis

First of, an overview into the various terminology will be given, which are relevant for this literature review. In the next chapter, the researched methodology is present. Then the most common data mining applications are classified and described, which are related in the different fraud detection areas. For that, literatures were analyzed and the best and most common application was chosen for this review. The basis for this literature review, the review from the authors Sharma, A., et. al. was used [1]. This review presents the different data mining techniques that are used for financial statement fraud. This study extends the financial fraud area on Insurance, Banking, Health and also Financial Statement fraud. After classification of the most common data mining application the results of the literature review is presented. A framework is developed to present the main objective included the fraud area, data mining application and data mining technique.

2. Terminology

2.1. Data Mining

While searching for the term "Data Mining" has been found, that for this term exist no clear definition in web. In fact, the term is not specific to a product, methodology technology or practice. According to the Gartner Group [2], "Data mining is the process of discovering meaningful new correlations, patterns and trends by sifting through large amounts of data stored in repositories, using pattern recognition technologies as well as statistical and mathematical techniques."

2.2.   Fraud

There is no existing a universal definition of fraud. The authors of the literature [2] describe different definitions of fraud. The first definition according the literature is from Oxford English Dictionary, which define fraud as „wrongful or criminal deception intended to result in financial or personal gain"[2]. The second definition mentioned is from Phua et al. who describe, "fraud as leading to the abuse of a profit organization's system without necessarily leading to direct leading consequences" [2].

2.3.   Financial Fraud

Same as fraud, there is no universal definition existing for financial fraud. Ngai. et. al. mention one definition in his paper from Wang et. al. which define financial fraud as "a deliberate act that is contrary to low, rule, or policy with intent to obtain unauthorized financial benefit."[2].

2.4.   Insurance Fraud

Insurance fraud is a process of financial fraud. It is also a popular researched area at the present. According to Legal Dictionary "Insurance Fraud occurs, when a person or entity makes false insurance claims in order to obtain compensation or benefits to which they are not entitled [3]. Ngai et. al. classify insurance fraud into three following categories: healthcare insurance fraud, crop insurance fraud and automobile insurance fraud [2].

2.5.   Bank Fraud

While searching for the definition of Bank fraud, has been found that there are also many words to define this type of fraud. The Legal Dictionary defines Bank Fraud as "The act of using illegal means to obtain money or other assets held by a financial institution."[4]. The statistic of published works shows that Bank Fraud is the most researched area [5]. The most common subcategory of Bank Fraud is credit card fraud.

3. Research methodology

To create this literature review on Data Mining techniques in fraud areas the following procedure was used. First, the topic was divided into individual keywords. Following keywords was used in this review to find the relevant literature: *Data Mining, Financial Fraud, Banking Fraud, Insurance Fraud, Healthcare Fraud, and Data mining techniques.* Only Journals from free available online databases was used. The search was restricted and used only the following online databases: Google Scholar, ScienceDirect and Springer Link.

To find the most relevant literatures the search in online databases was restricted to *Abstract, Title and Keywords.* Also, only those articles that had been published between 2010 and 2016 were selected and only those articles, which clearly described how the mentioned data mining techniques could be applied and assisted in frauds, were selected. The result of the literatures search showed, that there are total 10 articles found, which are most relevant for this literature review.

4. Classification of Data Mining Applications

In this chapter, the most common approaches of data mining applications classes are described. The following applications of data mining can handle different classes of problems.

Classification: Classification is the most commonly applied data mining technique, which employs a set of pre-classified examples to develop a model that can classify the population of records at large [6]. The literature research [7] says, that classification or prediction is the process of identifying a set of common features, and suggesting differentiating models that describe and distinguish data classes and concepts based on an example. The following example is very nice to understand ‚Classification' in easy words:

A loan creditor must analyze the data to determine which applicants are „safe" and which can be classified as „risky".

The most common data mining techniques for fraud detection are Neural Networks (NN), Naive Bayes, decision tress (DT) and also support vector machines (SVM).

Clustering: In Clustering, as known as cluster analysis the groups of objects, which have a similarity, are identified. The reason to choose the clustering procedure is, that some applications the class affiliation is not available or costly to identify [7]. So the task of Clustering is thus to assign the properties of a feature unclassified record a certain number of clusters [7]. Objects, which are not assigned here, can be assigned in the Data Mining class "outlier detection".
The goal of the cluster analysis is: "Classifying without knowing the classes prior".

The most common clustering techniques are neural networks, Naïve Bayes technique and K-nearest neighbor.

Regression: The goal if regression analysis is similar to the classification technique above. The difference is only that in regression no classes are formed. According to DMG this function is used to determine the relationship between the dependent variable and one or more independent variable [8].

Example:
From the data of a production facility has been recognized, that a certain product parameters correlated very strongly with product quality; now is to find out how these parameters must be set to achieve a specific level of quality [9].

Common Tools for *Regression* are linear regression and logistic regression.

Prediction: Prediction is similar to classification. The difference is, that in prediction the exception applies, the results lie in the future. For example, one possible question of prediction analysis would be: "How would be develop the dollar exchange rate in the future".

Neural networks and logistic model prediction are the most commonly used technique in prediction analysis.

Visualization: Visualization refers to presentation of data mining results so that the users can view complex view in the data as visual objects in dimensions and colors [10]. So it is easier for the users to understand the complicated data in clear patterns and use it. "Visualization helps business and data analysts to quickly and intuitively discover interesting patterns and effectively communicate these insights to other business and data analysts, as well as, decision makers [11]." Following visualization and presentation techniques provides this type of data mining technique: trees, tables, graphs, charts, matrices, crosstabs, curves or rules.

Outlier Detection: The aim of outlier detection is to identify data that are not compatible with rest of the dataset. It is one of the most fundamental issues in data mining. A commonly used technique for outlier detection is the discounting learning algorithm [2].

5. Literature Review

The authors of the first articles proposed a novel hybrid approach for under- sampling the majority class in largely skewed unbalanced datasets in order to improve the performance of classifiers [12]. For that, they used different Data mining techniques such as PNN, MLP, SVM, DT and GMDH to test the effectiveness of their approach [12]. The result shows that, by using DT and SVM on Insurance fraud detection achieved about 91% fraudulent claims detection rate (sensitivity). Against that GMDH achieved 81.3% sensitivity [12]. So it is clear that the proposed hybrid undersampling approach performed better than a original unbalanced data presented [12].

Bhowmik [13] present a confusion matrix of model applied to test data set. In his paper he provide a matrix with two classes with four possible outcomes of the classification to identify frauds. First is true positive, second false positive, third true negative and the last one false negative. To view and understand the output he recommends visualizing the output. For this, he proposes the following data mining techniques: Naïve Bayesian visualization to provide an interactive view of the prediction results [13]. Attribute columns graphs in neural networks to find the significant attributes and DT visualization to builds trees by splitting attributes from C4.5 classifiers [13].

This article [14] is about to develop a model for detecting cases of prescription fraud. A novel model is proposed for detecting cases of prescription fraud. Using a data mining approach dividing the six dimensional features into several 2 dimensional sub-domains [14]. The result is, that the automated fraud detection methodology gives considerably compatible results with the human expert auditing [14]. Based in the performance measurements with a true positive rate of 77.4 % and false positive rate of 6%, the developed system works good to detect prescription fraud problems [14].

The author of this article [15] performs an analysis using data mining methods to detect fraud in healthcare insurance. For the anomaly detection analysis he used the data mining technique SVM that is performed on an Oracle system. For the results he describe a data mining software that calculates the probability of the anomaly of each record [15]. If the probability from a claim header records greater than 50%, so the software marked the record as anomalous. For the analysis, the author presents 3 different criteria in this article. First criteria the Rejected claims, second the Excessive claims in health center types and the last Excessive claims in health centers.

Krivko [16] present a framework for a hybrid model based for plastic card fraud using supervised and unsupervised data mining techniques to identify fraudulent activity on the real debit card transaction data. The result was, that the hybrid model was more capable to identifying fraudulent activity in a timely manner than collaborating bank's existing rule-based system.

In this study [17] a transaction aggregation strategy was employed to detect credit card frauds. For the presentation of results, the authors used a classification table. The result in the table shows, that the employed model in this study predicted 1828 out 2420 fraudulent transactions as fraudulent (sensitivity 75,95%) [17]. Conclusion of this study was, that this study show the usefulness of creating derived attributes and reasonable data partitioning for fraud detection.

This study [18] use Bayesian Classification and Association Rule as DM techniques, to analyze and detect fraudulent account and the patterns of fraudulent transaction. A fraud detection system was developed based on six distinct signs were identified for the detection of fraudulent account using daily transaction data. Result of this study [18] was, that the developed system "… proposed more efficient and effective in detecting fraudulent accounts than manual screening" [18].

The goal of this study [19] is to analyze the performance this DM techniques: random forests, SVM together with logistic regression to identify credit card frauds. As classification this study use several measures, see also in literature [13]. Result shows, that Random forests demonstrated better performance across performance measure [19]. LR is according to this study, a commonly used standard technique of DM and has also performed good results.

This paper [20] present two data mining techniques, K-Means Clustering Algorithm and Multi-Level Feed Forward Network, to detect financial statement fraud. For analysis a dataset comprising of financial statements of companies are used. Algorithms such as PNN and MLFF are implemented on the dataset. Comparison of the results is made with the previous research. The results shows, that NNs are effective to predict the occurrence of fraudulent financial reporting [20].

The last study [21] used LR, CART and ANNs to sort out the different fraud factors in financial statement fraud. This research identifies fraud samples, which had been included in the prosecution and judgment cases [21]. For result, all the sample of datasets was divided randomly into the training dataset (70%) and testing dataset (30%) and selects 129 fraud cases and 447 non- fraud cases to test out the machine learning expert [T10]. Result of this study was, that ANN and CART approach achieve with a correct classification rate of 91,2% (ANN) and 90,4% (CART) in training sample and 92,8% (ANNs) and 90,3%(CART) in testing sample which is more exacter than logistic model (83,7%, 88,5%) [21].

Subsequently, the 10 relevant literatures are shown collectively in Table 3 below.

Ref.	Fraud Area	Data Mining Application	Data Mining Technique	Main Objective
[12]	Insurance Fraud, Banking Fraud	Classification	SVM, GMDH, PNN, MLP, DT, LR	To proposed a novel hybrid approach for detecting banking & insurance fraud
[13]	Insurance Fraud	Classification, Visualization, Prediction	Naive Bayes, DT, Bayesian Belief Networks	To predict and analyze fraud patterns from data.
[14]	Healthcare Fraud	Outlier detection	Supervised algorithms	To develop a model for detecting cases of prescription fraud
[15]	Healthcare Fraud	Anomaly detection, Clustering, Classification	SVM	To analyze fraud using Data mining methods in large data sets.
[16]	Banking Fraud	Classification	Supervised and unsupervised learning	To develop a framework for a hybrid model for plastic card fraud detection system.
[17]	Banking Fraud	Classification	LR	To detect credit card fraud transactions used a transaction aggregation strategy
[18]	Banking Fraud	Visualization, Presentation	Naive Bayes, Association Rule	To develop a fraudulent account detection system to assist the process of manual screening.
[19]	Banking Fraud	Classification	SVM, LR, Random forests	To examine the performance of two advanced data mining techniques; SVM, random forests and logistic regression for credit card fraud.
[20]	Financial Statement Fraud	Classification	NN (K-Means Clustering Algorithm and Multi-Level Feed Forward Network)	To employ a data mining framework for prevention and detection of financial statement fraud.
[21]	Financial Statement Fraud	Classification	LR, CART, ANN	To sort out the fraud factors and rank the importance of fraud factors using data mining techniques.

Table 1 - Research on data mining techniques in different fraud areas

9

6. Conclusion

This review presented literatures describing use of data mining applications and techniques for detecting frauds in Insurance, Healthcare, Banking and Financial Accounting areas. It transpired, that Neural Networks and Support Vector Machines are the most popular techniques of data mining to detect frauds in different types of fraud areas. All in all, the data mining technique NN was used in 5 of 10 searched literatures. Also SVM and LR were used in 4 papers to detect frauds and it noted that these techniques are very suitable to detect frauds. As basis, the literature review of Sharma, A., et. al. [literature review] was used and the results shows, that some data mining technique are no longer appeared in this paper, such as Fuzzy Logic, Genetic Algorithm and K-Nearest Neighbors. Remarkable in this study was, that the developed fraud detection systems are very close to the reality although, there are large amounts of data in some real-time are analyzed.

Financial Frauds detection using data mining techniques is a huge topic, which is still growing. For that reason, there should be more literatures about all kind of frauds. In this paper only Insurance, health, banking and financial fraud was reviewed, which have been published in the period from 2010 and 2016 and was restricted to Abstract, Title and Keywords. The future research could be about data mining technique in general fraud areas, which were not considered in this paper.

References

Print sources

[1] Sharma, A., Panigrahi, P.K., (2012) A Review of Financial Accounting Fraud Detection based on Data Mining Techniques, International Journal of Computer Applications, Vol. 39 No. 1, pp. 37-47

[2] E.W.T. Ngai et al., (2011) The application of data mining techniques in financial fraud detection: A classification framework and an academic review of literature, Decision Support Systems, p. 562.

[5] Abdallah A., et. al., (2016) Fraud detection system: A survey, Journal of Network and Computer Applications, pp. 90-113.

[6] Herbert A. Edelstein (1999) Introduction to Data Mining and Knowledge Discovery, Third Edition, Two Crows Corporation, pp. 10-11.

[7] Zhang, D., & Zhou, L. (2004). Discovering golden nuggets: data mining in financial application, IEEE Transactions on Systems, Man and Cybernetics 34 (4)

[9] Runkler, Thomas A. Data Mining : Methoden und Algorithmen intilligenter Datenanalyse (Computational Intilligence), Vieweg+Teubner Verlag; Auflage: 2010, p. 105

[10] Shaw, M. J., Subramaniam, C., Tan, G. W., & Welge, M. E. (2001). Knowledge management and data mining for marketing. Decision Support Systems, 31, pp.127-137.

[11] Soukup T., (2002) Visual Data Mining: Techniques and Tools for Data Visualization and Mining (Computer Science), John Wiley & Sons, 1, 5-6.

[12] Sundarkumer, G.G., Ravi. V., (2015) A novel hybrid undersampling method for mining unbalanced datasets in banking and insurance, Engineering Applications of Artificial Intelligence, Vol. 37, pp. 368–377.

[13] Bhowmik, R. (2011) Detecting Auto Insurance Fraud by Data Mining Techniques, Journal of Emerging Trends in Computing and Information Sciences, Vol. 2 No. 4, pp. 156-162.

[14] Aral, K.D., et. Al., (2012) A prescription fraud detection model, Computer Methods and Programs in Biomedicine, Vol. 106, pp. 37-46.

[15] Kirlidog, M., Asuk, C., (2012) A Fraud Detection Approach with Data Mining in Health Insurance, Procedia - Social and Behavioral Sciences, Vol. 62, pp. 989-994.

[16] Krivko, M. (2010) A hybrid model for plastic card fraud detection systems, Expert Systems with Applications, Vol. 37, pp. 6070–6076.

[17] Jha, S., et. al. (2012) Employing transaction aggregation strategy to detect credit card fraud, Expert Systems with Applications, Vol. 39, pp. 12650–12657.

[18] Wang, C., et. al. (2012) Identifying the signs of fraudulent accounts using data mining techniques, Computers in Human Behavior, Vol. 28, pp. 1002-1013.

[19] Bhattacharyya, S., et. al. (2011) Data mining for credit card fraud: A comparative study, Decision Support Systems, Vol. 50, pp. 602-613.

[20] Tangod, KK., et. al. (2015) Detection of Financial Statement Fraud using Data Mining Technique and Performance Analysis, International Journal of Advanced Research in Computer and Communication Engineering, Vol. 4, pp. 549-555.

[21] Lin, C.C., et. al. (2015) Detecting the financial statement fraud: The analysis of the differences between data mining techniques and experts' judgments, Knowledge-Based Systems, Vol. 89, pp. 459–470.

Internet sources

[2] http://www.gartner.com/it-glossary/data-mining/ , retrieved on 17th June 2016

[3] http://legaldictionary.net/insurance-fraud/ retrieved on 17th June 2016

[4] http://legaldictionary.net/bank-fraud/, retrieved on 17th June 2016

[8] http://dmg.org/pmml/v2-0/Regression.html, retrieved on 20th June 2016

YOUR KNOWLEDGE HAS VALUE

- We will publish your bachelor's and
  master's thesis, essays and papers

- Your own eBook and book -
  sold worldwide in all relevant shops

- Earn money with each sale

Upload your text at www.GRIN.com
and publish for free